Bikes Bombs and Baths

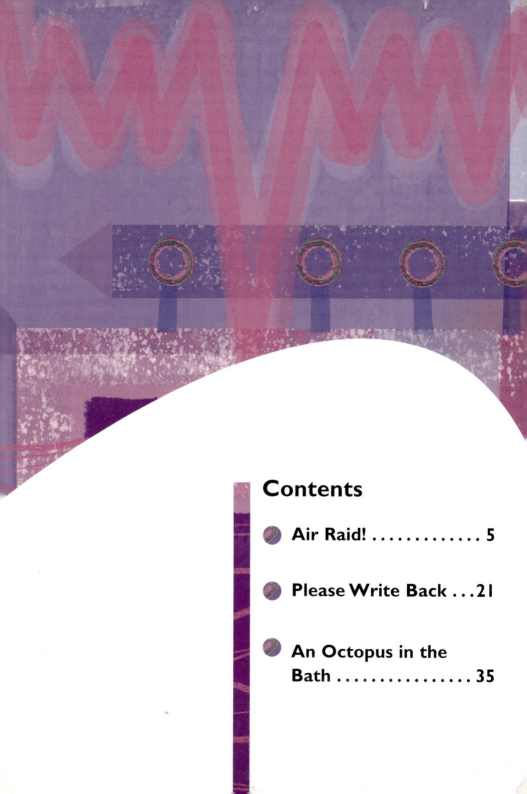

Contents

Rigby is an imprint of Pearson Education Limited, a company incorporated in England and Wales, having its registered office at Edinburgh Gate, Harlow,Essex,CM20 2JE
Registered company number: 872828

www.rigbyed.co.uk

Help and support for teachers, plus the widest range of education solutions

Rigby is a registered trademark of Reed Elsevier Inc, Licensed to Pearson Education Limited.

Bikes, Bombs and Baths first published 2004

'Air Raid!' © Harcourt Education Limited 2004

'Please Write Back' © Harcourt Education Limited 2004

'An Octopus in the Bath' © Harcourt Education Limited 2004

Series editor: Shirley Bickler

11

10 9

Bikes, Bombs and Baths
ISBN 978 0 433 03507 7

Group reading pack with teaching notes
ISBN 978 0 433 03563 3

Illustrated by Serina Curmi, Zara Merrick and Andy Hammond

Cover illustration © Max Ellis

Designed by StoreyBooks

Repro by Digital Imaging, Glasgow

Printed and bound in China (CTPS/09)

Air Raid!

written by Chris Buckton

illustrated by Serina Curmi

It was wartime and I was eight years old.
Everyone in our gang had bikes. Everyone,
except my friend Barry and me.

The gang didn't have new bikes. You
couldn't buy new bikes in the war because
nobody made them. Everybody was too busy
making bombs and aeroplanes. But all our
gang had second-hand bikes. All except
Barry and me.

Every night, we were left out while the gang rode up and down the street. We just stood by the lamp-post and watched.

Barry and I were saving up for a second-hand bike. We were going to share it. We were going to get the best bike in the world.

We saved our pocket money. We looked at the FOR SALE cards in the corner shop window.

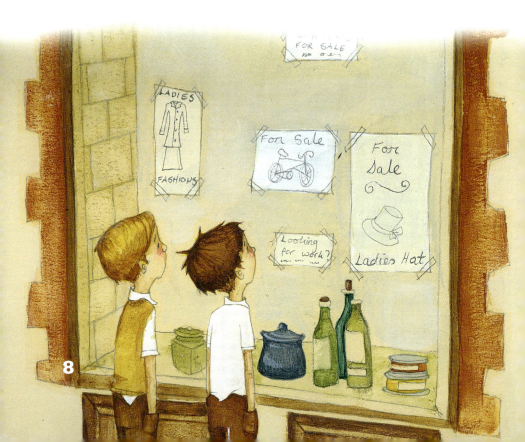

8

BARGAIN!
BOY'S BIKE
10/-

CLEARAN
shoes/dre
various

FOR SALE
Second-hand
bike £2

CHEAP
car engine

SALE
Used

For Sa
Men's cloth
All size

We even looked in the newspaper. But all of the bikes cost too much money. We only got 6d pocket money every week. It was going to take ages to save up.

9

Then one day, Barry came round to my house. He was riding … a BIKE! It had all the things a bike should have. All the things I dreamed of. It even had a dynamo and cable brakes. It was the best bike in the world.

"Blimey!" I said. "It's smashing! Can I have a go?"

Barry shook his head. "No. Sorry. My
cousin lent it to me."

I hated Barry then. How could he?
I thought we were going to share.

11

I watched him ride away. He was showing off – riding with no hands. I wanted him to fall off. He looked daft. I wouldn't care if his bike got smashed-up.

Later he rode off with the gang and I was the only one standing by the lamp-post. I wished that Barry would get smashed-up along with the bike.

That night there was an air raid and some families went down to the shelter in our street. Barry's family always went there, but my family sat under the stairs. If our house got hit, Mum reckoned the stairs would save us.

We were used to the bombs now, but this air raid was scary. The bombs seemed very close. They made a horrible thumping noise. The walls wobbled and dust fell on us, but the stairs didn't fall down. Our house was safe.

14

In the morning when the air raid was over, I went out into our street. The corner shop had been hit by a bomb. The shop had no walls left and we could see inside as if it was a doll's house. I could see the counter covered in dust and bricks. There was a huge hole where the door had been.

And … there was a bike outside the shop. The wheel was sticking out from a pile of bricks. It was smashed-up.

It was Barry's bike. I smiled. Barry's fancy bike was wrecked. It served him right. Then I stopped smiling. Where was Barry?

I looked at the smashed-up bike. I called his name. Was Barry's body under the bricks? Was it smashed-up like the bike? I started to pull bricks away from the bike.

"Barry! Barry!" I was crying. What if he was dead? It was my fault. I had wished that he would die.

Then I heard a voice. "What are you doing?"

It was Barry! He was alive! He was just standing there! I punched him and he punched me and we both started laughing.

18

"The bike's had it!" he said. "It's all smashed-up. I had to leave it outside the shop when we went to the air raid shelter. My cousin will murder me."

I never told him I had wished that he would get smashed-up too. I'm glad he didn't.

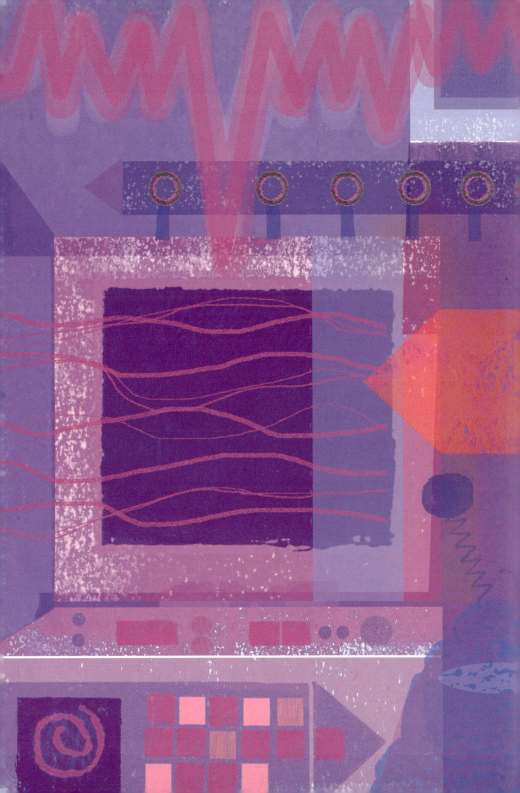

Please Write Back

written by Chris Buckton

illustrated by Zara Merrick

Dear Mum

We got here late. It was dark. I'm staying on a farm. I hate it. There's Mr and Mrs Brown and David. He's 9. I hate him. I'll tell you all the things I hate.

I hate David. He wanted me to be a boy.

I hate the food. We had rice pudding. There was brown skin on it. Mrs Brown said that was the best bit. I said it was horrible.

I hate the toilet. It's OUTSIDE and it's like a bucket. There's no light. I can feel spider webs on my face. I HATE IT.

There are no shops. Mrs Brown said Woolworths is 30 miles away. There's no fish and chip shop.

I want to come home. I miss you. Give Gran a hug from me.

Love from
Maggie

PS Please write back.

PPS Please send me a battery for my torch.

Dear Maggie

It was lovely to get your letter and to know you're all right. I'm sure you'll get used to things. Do try and be a good girl and not upset everybody. The bombs are really bad here. Fifteen planes came over last night. Dad says there were lots of fires started. So it's best you're safe in the country.

I'm sending you a vest to keep you warm. I made it out of Dad's old one. I hope it fits.

We miss you and all your noise!

Lots of love

Mum

25

Dear Mum

This farm is mucky. The cows just poo in the field and it stinks. There's a carthorse. It's HUGE. David said I could sit on it. I said, "not blooming likely."

The cat had kittens. They just popped out and the cat licked them. DISGUSTING.

Mr Brown kills the hens. He grabs hold and wrings their necks. It's cruel. The hens squawk like mad.

Mrs Brown makes me eat my greens. She says if you eat carrots you can see in the dark. I said, "tell me another one."

Love from
Maggie

PS The vest was too small so I put it in the kittens' bed.

PPS We had roast chicken. It was yummy.

PPPS Please write back.

Dear Maggie

I do hope you're not being rude to Mrs Brown. Try and eat everything up like a good girl. Lucky you, having roast chicken. We're stuck with spam, spam, and more spam! But I got a real orange yesterday – I had to queue for 2 hours!

I do worry about you. Keep smiling. Let's hope you'll be back home soon. The raids are still bad. We've been down the shelter every night this week.

I'm making you a blouse out of Aunty's old frock. Pink suits you and you'll look a real lady in it!

Lots of love

Mum

Dear Mum

Sorry I haven't written.

Don't bother about the blouse. Mrs Brown gave me David's old overalls so I can go in the muck.

Guess what? Mr Brown gave me a bit of garden. I've sown some lettuce and radishes and carrots.

Here is a plan of my garden.

Love
Maggie

Dear Maggie

Fancy you growing lettuce. I thought you didn't like greens!! You sound like a proper country girl. We all miss you. Gran says the house isn't the same without you carrying on!

There was no bombing this week. Maybe we'll be able to come and fetch you home.

Lots of love

Mum

PS Please write back.

31

Dear Mum

I want to stay here FOR EVER.

Love from
Maggie

Dear Mr and Mrs Brown and David

Thank you for having me. And thank you for the kitten. We went to Woolworths on Saturday to get it a collar.

Lots of love
Maggie

PS Here's a photo of me in my new blouse.

PPS I'll never forget you.

PPPS Please write back.

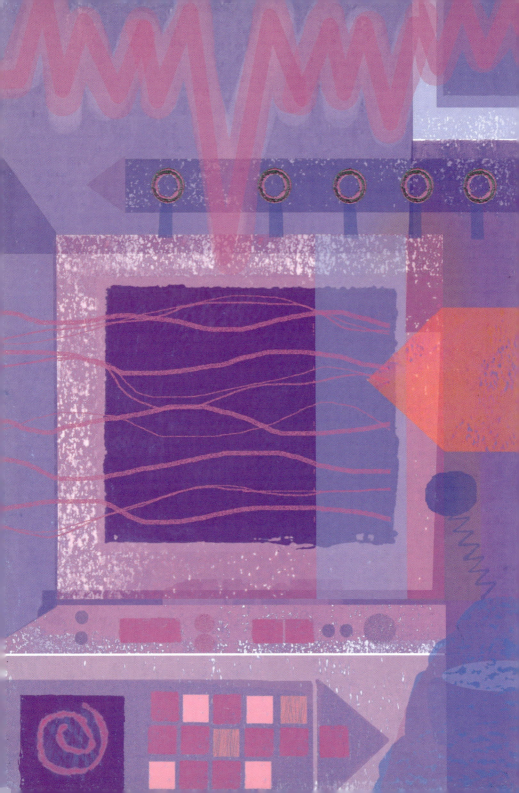

An Octopus in the Bath

written by Ann Jungman

illustrated by Andy Hammond

Setting the Scene

The story takes place in a Roman villa near Hadrian's Wall in the north of England. The wall was built by the Romans to keep out the barbarians who lived further north. The villa has a new bathhouse, rather like a small swimming pool.

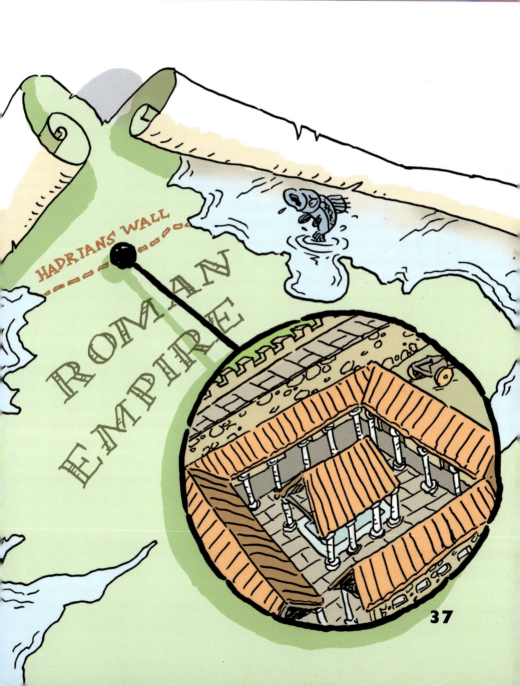

Characters

Grattus

Helfur

Narrator

Scene

one

Narrator   *The family is watching Grattus make*
a mosaic on the bottom of the pool.

Grattus   Sir, I've nearly finished the bath.
What sort of picture would you like
in the middle?

Horatio   What do you think, dear?

Diana   Oh, something that reminds us of the
sea near Rome.

Grattus   Well, Madam, I find that many Roman ladies go for dolphins.

Diana   Oh yes, a dolphin would be charming.

Narrator   *Peculia and Muckus peer over the edge of the pool.*

Horatio   Keep away from the edge of the pool, children. It's deep and it's empty – you'd get a nasty bang if you fell in.

Muckus   (*pulling a face*) Is Grattus really going to put a *dolphin* down there?

Diana   What's wrong with a dolphin?

Muckus   It's boring.

Horatio   Well, what would you like?

Muckus   (*waving his arms*) What about a sixteen-armed octopus?

Diana   Who'd want to get into a pool with an octopus on the bottom?

Muckus and Peculia (*shouting*) We would!

43

Horatio   Don't be silly, children.
Grattus, get going
on the dolphin
tomorrow.

Grattus   Right you are, Sir.
I'll just cut up the
coloured pieces
for the mosaic
today, and I'll start
on the dolphin
tomorrow.

Diana   Excellent, I can't wait. Oh, we'll have
the most elegant bathhouse in the
north of England. The neighbours will
be so jealous.

Muckus   I'm not getting into a bath with a boring old dolphin.

Peculia   Nor am I.

Horatio   You'll do as you are told or I will punish you. Children today! No discipline. I don't know what the world is coming to. I'd never have spoken to my parents like that.

Scene

two

Narrator *That night, in the pitch dark, Muckus and Peculia creep into the bathhouse. Peculia is carrying a big bag.*

Muckus It's so dark, Peculia, I can hardly see a thing.

Peculia There's no moon. That's why.

Muckus How are we going to make an octopus in the bath if we can't see?

Peculia (*holding up her bag*) I've brought candles and oil lamps. Let's get into the pool and light them.

47

Narrator *The children clamber into the pool and make a circle of light around them.*

Muckus Where shall we start?

Peculia I've got some charcoal. I'll draw the outline and then we can fill it in with mosaic pieces.

Muckus I'm not sure this is such a brilliant idea anymore, Peculia. Mother and Father will go mad when they see it.

Peculia No way! The octopus will be fantastic! They'll love it.

Muckus   Are you sure?

Peculia   Sure, I'm sure. Now here goes. I'll draw a big bulging body in the middle.

Muckus   It looks a bit odd.

Peculia   It'll be fine once we put his legs on. Here's a bit of charcoal – you do eight tentacles that side and I'll do eight on this side.

Narrator *The children work for hours, until sixteen long tentacles cover the floor of the bath.*

Muckus This is hard work, Peculia. I'm starving.

Peculia You're in luck. I took some food when I pinched the candles. Let's see. Ah yes, I've got stuffed dormice and larks' tongues in honey. Which do you want?

Muckus What, no snails?

Peculia   Sorry.

Muckus   All right, I'll have the stuffed dormice then. (*Stuffs them into his mouth*) Oh yum, are there any more?

Peculia   No. Now let's get on with this octopus. Let's stick the mosaic pieces in place.

Muckus   It's not as easy as it looks, Peculia, and this octopus is ugly and scary. Mother will be furious.

Peculia   Yes, but I bet Father will really like it.

Muckus   Well, I hope you're right or we'll be in real trouble.

Peculia   Look! It's a bit creepy. When the
candles flicker it looks as if
it's moving!

Muckus   (*in a spooky voice*)
Maybe it's coming alive …

Peculia   Be quiet, Muckus,
I can hear
something.

Muckus   (*joking*) Yes – my
knees knocking
when I think how angry Mother and
Father will be.

Peculia   No, you idiot, I really can hear
something. Listen.

Narrator   *After a few seconds …*

Muckus   (*whispering*) I think there's someone on the roof.

Peculia   It must be the barbarians from the other side of the wall. They always attack on dark nights, when there is no moon. Oh Muckus, I'm scared.

Muckus   Me too. We've got to warn Father.

Peculia   You creep out and sound the alarm. I'll stay here and sing loudly so they don't hear you go.

Muckus   Will you be all right on your own? I don't like to leave you.

Peculia It's our only hope. If you don't wake up the household the barbarians will kill us all. Now, go and get help!

Muckus All right. Good luck, Peculia. Start singing now.

Narrator *Muckus creeps out. Peculia sings at the top of her voice.*

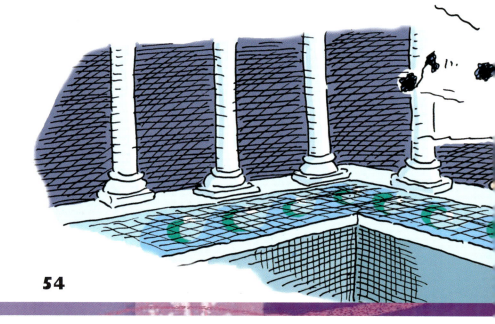

Peculia Octopus, octopus,

What a fine piece of art you are.

Octopus, octopus,

Oh, how you will please my mama.

Octopus, octopus,

What a base to a bath.

Octopus, octopus,

Oh, how my father will laugh.

55

Scene

three

Narrator   *Five minutes later, the lights go on in the house and a gong booms loudly.*

Peculia   Great, Muckus has told Father.

Narrator   *At that moment a huge hairy man jumps in through the roof and grabs Peculia. He puts his dagger to her throat.*

Helfur   (*hissing*) Not a sound or I'll slit your throat.

57

Peculia   Oh, please don't hurt me. My father will be here in a minute. If you harm me you'll be in trouble.

Helfur   What! You think I'm scared of some Roman? Ha, you don't know me. I'm Helfur the Warrior!

Narrator   *Helfur raises his dagger to stab Peculia. Suddenly, he staggers back, covering his eyes with his arm. He has seen the octopus on the bottom of the bath.*

Helfur   (*terrified*) Aaargh! What is that evil creature? What is that monster from hell?

Peculia   It is an evil sea creature that attacks people who harm Roman girls.

Octopus, octopus,
Lying on the ground.
Octopus, octopus,
Get this man bound.

Helfur   No! No! Spare me.
It has so many
arms! It is terrible!

Narrator   *Horatio, Diana and Muckus rush in.*

Horatio   (*waving his sword*) Drop your dagger, villain, and let my daughter come to me.

Narrator *The barbarian is cowering in a corner of the bath, shaking with terror. Peculia climbs out of the bath and throws herself into her mother's arms.*

Horatio In the name of the gods, what is going on here?

Peculia It's all right, Father, he's terrified of our octopus.

Diana Our *what?*

Muckus The octopus Peculia and I made on the floor of the bath.

Horatio Well, thank the gods you made such a beast. You seem to have saved us all. Now, you, barbarian. You came to my house and attacked my family in the dark of night. You deserve to die.

Narrator *Horatio draws his sword and jumps into the bath.*

Helfur (*begging*) Don't throw me to the evil many-legged monster!

Horatio If I spare you, will you take your men and go?

Helfur   You have my word as a warrior. We will go back to our side of the wall.

Horatio   Go, then. Tell your tribe about our monster and never come back to my house. If you do, the octopus will rise up and eat you in one gulp.

Helfur   W...w...we shall never return, Roman, never.

Narrator   *The terrified barbarian climbs out of the bath and runs off calling for his men. He doesn't look back.*

Diana   Oh, Peculia, my baby, how brave you were. We are so proud of you.

Horatio Never mind that. What exactly is that mess down there, you two? And just what were you doing in the bathhouse in the middle of the night?

Peculia and Muckus Well you see, Father, it was like this …